CHAPTER 2

Cinderella

Illustrated by László Gál

Once upon a time there lived a girl.
The girl was very good and kind.
But the girl had two very mean stepsisters.
They made her work all the time.

All day long the girl cleaned the house.
All night long the girl swept the fireplace.
The girl was always covered with ashes.
Her stepsisters laughed at her and called her
Cinderella.

One day, Cinderella's family received
an invitation.
Everyone was invited to a royal ball.

"What shall we wear?" the stepsisters giggled.

They ran up to their rooms.

"I would like to go to the ball," said Cinderella.

The stepsisters laughed and laughed.

"You cannot go in those dirty rags," they said.
"And you must finish cleaning the house, too."

Cinderella sat down and cried.
But then a fairy appeared.

"I am your fairy godmother," the fairy said.
"Anything you wish for will come true."

Ping! Pang! Poof! Cinderella had a new dress.
Ping! Pang! Poof! Cinderella had glass slippers.

"Thank you, fairy godmother," Cinderella said
as she left for the ball.

Cinderella arrived at the ball.
She was the most beautiful girl there.
Cinderella's stepsisters were there.
They did not even know that the beautiful
girl was Cinderella.

The prince asked Cinderella to dance.
"I would love to," said Cinderella.

They danced and talked and laughed.
The prince and Cinderella fell in love.

Cinderella was very happy.
But she knew the fairy's magic would not last.
She kissed the prince and ran away.
As she ran, Cinderella lost one of her glass slippers.

The prince ran after Cinderella.
But he could not catch her.
Then he found her glass slipper.

"I must find her," said the prince.
"She is my one true love."

The prince set out to visit every home in his kingdom.
But he could not find anyone who fit the glass slipper.

Finally the prince arrived at Cinderella's house.
The sisters made Cinderella hide.
Then they tried on the glass slipper.
They squeezed and struggled, but the slipper
did not fit.

The prince heard someone in another room.

"Who is that?" the prince asked.

"That's just our sister, Cinderella,"
said the sisters.
"She was not at your royal ball," they added.

"Bring her here," the prince said.

Cinderella's clothes were dirty and torn.
But the prince did not mind.
The slipper fit Cinderella and he knew he had
found his love.

That very day, Cinderella and the prince were married.
And they lived happily ever after.